Hermetics And The Mental Body

A. S. Raleigh

LESSON III

THE MENTAL BODY

In the first place, you must be able to conceive of mind being separated and apart from thoughts. The great trouble in all investigations along this line is that people confuse mind and thought. You must conceive mind as existing before any thinking took place. This may sound very coarse and gross to some of you; you have been taught that mind is the highest activity of the soul. It is material, nevertheless, which I will endeavor to show you before we get through. Mind is the highest aspect of thought, and when you understand this you are then able to understand the relation of all those things. Now, this may sound to you at first to be not very definite, but as a matter of fact there is nothing any more far-reaching than this statement.

Mind is the material of which thought is made. Mind is one of the planes of nature. If there were not a man in the world there would still be mind; if there were nothing created, no object created, yet there still would be mind. Mind is the mental substance, that force which exists in the world without. It is one of the aspects of the world.

We have five octaves of vibration in Nature, namely, the Spiritual, the Buddhic, the Mental, the Astral, and the Physical. First, there is the physical octave, covering the vibrations which manifest as the undifferentiated Ether, in its positive and negative differentiations of electricity and magnetism, together with the earth, air, fire and water, or in modern technical terminology, carbon, nitrogen, oxygen and hydrogen, positive and negative activities of these two principles.

(23)

Then, there is, second, the astral octave, which includes also life, which we learned about in the last lesson; and there is the mental octave, and there are two octaves above the mental plane.

The Mental Octave includes seven notes of vibration. The four lower notes of this octave are devoted to the region of concrete thought, the three higher notes are in the region of abstract thought, making the Septenary of the Mental Octave. This must sound like attenuated moonshine, and yet it is exact science.

You will find that there is a perfect harmony and perfect relation working all the way through. Now, mind movements express themselves in atoms, that is, ultimate atoms, electrons and molecules that are gathered together by reason of a harmonious rate of vibration expressed in rhythm; and simple thought is an organism formed by a movement of the atoms of mind; that is, mental atoms being drawn together by a common rate of vibration, they are held together and thus form an organism. A compound thought is a number of these thoughts, which are drawn together and held in position by a common chord and form a compound organism; a complex thought is a number of these compound thoughts drawn together and are dominated by a common tone, thereby being held together so as to form a complex thought structure; a thought form is a mass of mental matter ensouled by complex thoughts; which is being taught in our lessons on Motion and Number. That is, in the lesson on the Rhythm of Mind, which is the seventh lesson. These matters are made plainer in some respects there than at present we have time for.

The thing I must impress upon your intelligence is that mind is force, separate and apart from thought; thought is an organism which is developed as a result of this mental activity. Now, remember, therefore, that mind exists separate and apart from thought, and it may astonish you when we enunciate this so often, but this is something that scientists, psychologists, in the past have denied. The fundamental principle of the schools in the past was to deny that thought was a thing, to deny that it had any existence; only that it was a kind of condition, not a thing. Thought has a tangible existence; it is a material substance. Rather, mind, of which thought is composed, is a material substance. Now, the brain has been developed for the express purpose of expressing thought; in other words, mental matter acts through the tissue of the brain, and it is so developed as to offer the requisite degree of resistance to enable mind to express itself in thought. The different classes of vibration must have groups of mental matter, fibre and cells adapted to respond to that particular rhythm into combination of vibration, and as the class to which a thought belongs always coincides with the class of vibration to which it belongs, thus rates of vibration express themselves in thoughts; in other words, that organism will express itself in the faculty pertaining to it.

Not only is this true, but each cell is developed and has a certain vibratory relation and vibratory capacity, which will express itself in that way, and the various brain fibres are trained and have that relation, that vibratory capacity, so that they will respond to that rate of vibration, and thus express themselves in that thought. The brain is merely the organism established by nature for the purpose of expressing itself in vibratory activity. Remember that it is but the physical organism for the activity of the mind. Now, as the mind expresses itself through that organism, that being its center of activity, and expressing itself through that; in other words, thought coming into manifestation according as it brings itself into that vibratory expression, what is the inevitable result? Simply this: that thought is an organism, a being, a body, when it is expressing itself in this way. It should be borne in mind, that as mind, expressing itself through thought, is being generated, it flows outward from its center, forming a kind of sphere, in one sense of the word, which it will express or manifest, when it thus forms a body (and this is the origin of the expression "Mental Body"). In this way we get the idea of mind expressing itself as a body, as another principle in the human constitution.

It is only when we realize this, that mind exists as a body, as another principle in the human constitution and not merely as a kind of visionary something we don't know what, (the way the most of the physicists would have us to believe); it is in this way that we can see real truth.

Now, the mind force forms a body, which entirely permeates the astral body and goes on down to the etheric double, and in the course of time to the physical body. There is nowhere where mind is not present. Remember that mind is the principle of Man, where it transcends the astral principle and rises above to the soul, or Buddhi, and expresses itself through the brain. What then are we to understand in relation to the mind? You know it has been the theory for a very long time among psychologists and mental physiologists, that mind was related to the genus Homo, and they supposed that nobody but Man was in possession of Mind. This is not true, for mind is a principle of Nature, and extends to the Animal, Vegetable, and even to the Mineral kingdoms; Man's mind being different only in degree to all the other beings in this respect.

Schopenhauer makes this very clear, and shows, that in nature, Will is manifested among animals and also among plants. The bean vine illustration, in which he shows the Will in Nature, covers this illustration of Will in the Vegetable kingdom. The radical of a bean, in its efforts to reach the surface of the earth, came in contact with a shoe sole, and it couldn't get through; there were forty thread holes. It divided itself into forty filaments and passed through the thread holes, and then united again, and went to the surface, and made a stalk of beans. It was only when digging in the ground, that they discovered how the plant had figured it all out and had decided just what had to take place. This is not instinct; instinct does not stimulate any such intelligence as that. Any plant will seek the light no matter where it is; not only is that true, but climbing plants will go through crevices, go over walls and hunt for a place, where they can attach themselves. They really hunt for those places. Therefore, we find in the plant world abundant evidence of intelligence, not instinct. Not only is this true, but Darwin's work on Vegetable Mold, shows, that earth worms have the capacity to learn by experience. If they do learn, they must have the reasoning faculties. You may go wherever you please; you will find that plants and animals have reasoning faculties. It naturally follows, that those states of existence have Mind just as much in the absolute as Man has, though least in degree; that is the only difference—least in degree. Now, the Mind is not purely a human activity, a human achievement, but is something which is universally applicable throughout nature. All forms of life, or forms of existence are in possession of this power, namely Mind. It is manifesting itself through all the activities of life. Now, as a matter of fact, Mind expresses itself through this

Mental body (The mental body is the form which mind takes in its activities) permeating the astral body.

As we said before, the highest three notes of the mental octave express themselves in abstract thought. Now, what is the result? There are two distinct bodies formed. One is formed by concrete thought and is formed out of the four lower notes of the mental octave: the other is formed out of abstract thought and is the result of activities of abstract thinking; and represents the triad, the three higher notes of the mental octave. This is ordinarily called "the causal body." All the concrete activities are the result of abstract mental activity; all these abstract mental activities act through the causal body. Now, when you stop to think, it is a fact that only a small per cent of the human race think in the abstract, and you may readily see the causal body is relatively weak in comparison to the mental body. When a man dies, his astral body leaves the physical behind, and goes out into the astral plane, and in time his mental body goes out into the mental plane abandoning the astral, and in time his causal body leaves the mental body. It is generally claimed by Theosophy, that it is a fact that the soul ultimately leaves the causal body.

There is no evidence of immortality offered by any kind of Spiritual phenomena. There is one death on the astral plane and two deaths on the mental plane. After the physical death, there is no evidence of perpetuity of existence; therefore, it does not prove these things. We mean both the lower mental body and, also, the causal body in contra-distinction from the physical and astral.

Now all concrete thought goes to build up this concrete vehicle, the mental body; all abstract thought builds up the abstract vehicle, the causal body. Whenever we are thinking along those lines we are exercising an influence along that direction; wherever we turn we are doing that kind of work.

The Mental Body is yellow; the Causal Body approaches the gold in its color, just as the Astral Body is some shade of blue. The Etheric Double is pink, or rather the color of fresh blown peach blossoms. Red is positive or masculine; blue on the astral plane indicates the feminine; the red indicates a preponderance of masculinity no matter where it may be. Now, on through each of the bodies there is a certain state of consciousness corresponding to the particular principle involved. The mental consciousness is primarily the super-consciousness. It is possible to leave the astral body behind entirely in addition to the physical and go out in the mental body to travel on the mental plane. The astral activity is not the only one which transcends the physical, for it is possible for us to rise above the astral into the mental and carry on those activities; no question about it, it is possible to do it. We have done it ourselves. The mental body is the highest aspect of what might properly be termed Mind. The soul and the spirit are the two forces above the mental body. The mental body functions the various centers, and has as its center the brain, just as the astral body, the heart; the prana, the solar plexus and the etheric body the spleen.

You may see the mental body projected; both may be projected as the case may be. The color of the causal body may be some shade of gold, while the color of the mental body will be some shade of yellow, but not golden.

As the various thoughts cannot express themselves until they meet resistance through the tissue, the tissue must offer resistance in order that they may express themselves; all manifestations are due to resistance. Now, suppose there is no brain fibre and no brain cells

which have the same key-notes which the thought has;
they will not resist it, but it will go right through them,
and no resistance will be offered. There is a continual
tendency to alter the tissue in accordance with the vibration which has to pass through it, so that in time that
tissue is so modified that it will resist, it will acquire
that rate of vibration, and so will resist that vibration
of the mind and the result is, there will be a new brain
fibre, and new brain cells develop, or else the brain cells
will be modified so that they will respond to that activity, and then that thought will be able to manifest itself.

You understand that the mental process is the process
of the "ever-becoming;" it is not stationary in any
sense whatever, but is going through a continual process
of evolution, and this is the process of the "Ever-becoming," So as the cells strive to adapt themselves to
new conditions, they will assume new vibratory relations,
vibratory capacities; and assuming these, they will express themselves in certain ways. Now, it is true those
capacities, those vibratory activities, expressing themselves in those different ways, constitute the true founda-
tions upon which our mental progress really depends.
All the way through it is a progress of the "ever-becoming" and those vibratory expressions organize brain
fibres and brain cells to properly express themselves; that
is really the truth. It is a new organism of tissue which
is adapted to the expression of that impulse. And bear
in mind, this complex brain structure is merely the in-
strument which the mind is employing to enable it to
manifest itself in thought; it being the physical organ
of the mental body.

CPSIA information can be obtained
at www.ICGtesting.com
Printed in the USA
LVRC030537050920
665109LV00005B/20

9 781163 051023